trouble dolls

dolls

A Guatemalan Legend

By Suzanne Simons

Illustrated by Diego Isaias Hernández Mendez

◣SCHOLASTIC

New York Toronto London Auckland Sydney
Mexico City New Delhi Hong Kong

ISBN 0-439-15415-4

Published by Scholastic Inc.
SCHOLASTIC and associated logos are trademarks
and/or registered trademarks of Scholastic Inc.

a book soup book

12 11 10 9 8 7 6 5 4 3 2 1

Printed in Singapore.
First Scholastic printing, February 2000

Contents

the legend of
the trouble dolls

There are many mysterious things in the land of Guatemala.

Some say that if you travel into the hills and tell your troubles to the sky at dusk, you will dream of the answers when you go to sleep that night. Some also say that if you tell the sky your secret wishes, the wind will whisper in your ear how to make those wishes come true.

But those stories are just legends, stories that were told to young children to help them get to sleep. They are ancient myths. We all know that neither the sky nor the wind has secret magical powers.

Because in Guatemala, the magical powers are in the cloth that the people weave.

Once upon a time, in the hills of Guatemala, there lived a Maya woman with two children. The woman's husband had died many years earlier. So now they lived alone in a small hut.

The woman's name was Flora, and she was a weaver. Every day she worked on rolls and rolls of beautiful cloth. The sky was her

inspiration. When the sun rose, she wove cloth with bright yellows and reds and greens. In the middle of the day she wove cloth with pure light blues and whites and pinks. At sunset she wove cloth with reds and oranges and purples. And at night she wove cloth of deep, deep blacks and forest greens with white stripes for the shooting stars. She kept the cloth she had woven in a large basket made of cactus strands.

Her children, Diego and Maria, went to school in the nearby village. They woke up very early every day to help with chores. They tended to the small, dry field on which they tried to grow their food. After school, they helped their mother. Twice a week, they all took the wonderful cloth to market, carrying it on their backs, with straps around their heads.

The children were happy most of the time. They sang to each other. They told stories. They played games and talked and drew pictures when they weren't working in the field or helping with chores.

But there was one problem—the family was very, very poor. The rain had not come for months, and the field was empty. And their mother could not make enough cloth to keep food on their plates. They ate corn tortillas and beans for almost every meal, because that was all they could afford.

The whole family slept in the same room, in hammocks. At night Maria would try to scare her brother by shaking his hammock with her feet. "There is a robber in the house!" he would cry, only to hear his sister laughing to herself. She fooled him every time.

One night, Diego felt his hammock shaking. *She's doing it again,* he thought. *I'll get her this time.* Diego sat up straight. He turned around and yelled, "Booooo!" right in his sister's face. At least, that was what he planned to do. What really happened was that he found himself face-to-face with a real robber who was holding all his mother's cloth!

The robber ran out immediately, taking the cloth with him. Maria and her mother awakened. "What happened?" Flora asked.

"A ma—a man …" Diego paused to catch his breath. "A man came in and ran off with your cloth!"

Flora began to sob. "That was six months' worth of work he stole."

None of them slept for the rest of the night, in fear that the robber would return.

The robber had stolen every bit of cloth that Flora had made! The market was the very next day, and they had nothing to sell! Flora cried and cried in despair. She was in her hammock when Maria and Diego left for school in the village.

When they returned, Flora was still in her hammock, now sick with fever. "We must help Mama," Maria said. So Maria and Diego searched through the basket to see if there was anything left to sell. All they found were scraps—tiny, useless bits of cloth of all shapes and sizes and colors that didn't match at all.

Then Maria had an idea. She and Diego gathered the scraps. They went outside and picked up as many twigs as they could.

They worked all afternoon and all night. "What are you doing?" Flora asked from her hammock.

"It's a secret," said Maria. And they kept on working.

When they were done, they had made dozens of tiny dolls! There were little men and little women. Each wore different pieces of clothing, depending upon the scraps that were available. And Diego and Maria had made little pouches for the dolls to sleep in—six per pouch. They had used every scrap of cloth in the house. The dolls were all they could hope to sell at the market.

As Maria looked proudly over their work, she remembered a story she had once been told when she was very, very young. It was about a magical doll who granted its owner several wishes. She thought that it was just a story— but maybe, just maybe, it could be true! So that night, before bed, Maria selected her favorite pouch—a lovely purple, pink, and green one. She went outside and removed the dolls. She held them in

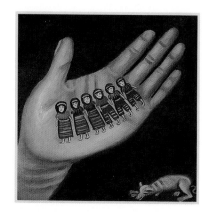

the palm of her hand and spoke to each of them.

"Good night, my little friends. We have many problems, and I need your help. Our fields are dry and barren. My mother is ill. We have no food. Our beautiful cloth was stolen. So please, little dolls, help us if you can. Tomorrow is market day, and if we do not sell our crafts we will go hungry."

And with that, Maria placed each of the dolls back in the pouch and then put the pouch on the windowsill.

The next morning, Maria woke up as the sunlight shined into her eyes. She looked at the windowsill and saw a very strange sight. The dolls were outside the pouch, lying in a little circle on the windowsill! *I'm certain I put them back in the pouch last night,* Maria thought. *Maybe I only imagined I did.* She scratched her head, gathered the dolls, placed them in the bag with the other dolls, and got dressed.

After breakfast, Maria and Diego set off for the market, carrying a large cloth bag full of the dolls. Flora, still sick, got herself up for the first time and waved to them weakly from the door. "Good luck, my children," she called after them as they walked down the road. *"Buena suerte!"*

When they arrived at the market, it was already bustling with merchants setting up their stands. They went to their mother's usual spot, next to Rafael, the shoe seller.

"Where is your beautiful cloth today?" Rafael asked.

"It was taken from us," Diego explained. Maria laid out a blanket on the ground. Diego poured the pouches of dolls out. "This is all we have to sell today," he said. He held up the dolls for Rafael to see.

Rafael snickered. "Who would want something so small?"

"We shall see," said Maria. "There is magic in these dolls."

"There is magic in these shoes, too," Rafael mocked. "But that won't help them sell."

"We shall see, we shall see," said Maria.

When the market opened, their hopes were high. People came from the surrounding villages to buy supplies—food, clothing, tools, everything.

But no one was buying the dolls.

"Do you have any cloth today?" an old woman asked. *"No, abuela,"* said Maria. "But we have these magic dolls." The old woman just waved her hand and walked off.

At midday, Rafael the shoe seller had sold nearly all of his shoes. Pedro the fish man had sold almost all of his fish. Rosa the fruit lady had sold almost all of her fruit.

But Maria and Diego had sold not one set of dolls.

Finally, the sun began to set. Market day was just about over. Maria and Diego were extremely sad—they had not sold one pouch of dolls.

"I guess my wishes didn't work," said Maria to no one in particular.

"What?" asked Diego.

"Nothing," said Maria as she began to put away the dolls.

Just then, a man in a straw hat, dressed in fine clothes, approached Maria and Diego. He had a gentle smile. In a very

deep voice, he said, "What are you selling, children?"

"Not much," said Diego. "No one has bought anything."

"Show me," the man said.

Diego opened a pouch. He poured the dolls into the man's hand. They tumbled and seemed to dance as they landed.

"They are just dolls," Diego said.

"No, not just dolls," said Maria. "*Magical* dolls."

The man furrowed his already wrinkled brow. He removed his hat and scratched his head. "Magical, eh? I could use a bit of magic." He took out a wad of money. "I'll take them all." He handed them enough money to feed a family for a year!

"Let me get you change," said Maria, excitedly. She and Diego turned to ask the shoe seller if he had change, but he had left.

And when they turned around, the mysterious man had vanished as well, taking the dolls with him.

Maria and Diego ran home to find their mother up and making dinner.

"Mama! Mama! Look!" cried Diego, holding the money for her to see.

Flora could not believe her eyes. "How did you make so much? We had nothing to sell!" she said.

"Yes, we did," said Diego. "We sold magic."

"Magic?" asked Flora. "What do you mean?"

They went inside, and Maria told her mother everything. She told her how they made the dolls, how Maria spoke to them at night, and how the mysterious man bought every single pouch!

"It does not sound much like magic to me," said Flora. "It sounds like my children worked very hard."

"But how do you explain the fact that you are feeling better now?" asked Maria.

"That is the way trouble is," Flora explained. "It comes and then it goes."

"And what about the rain?" Diego asked.

Maria and Flora turned to him. "What rain?" they said together.

"*That* rain," Diego said, pointing outside.

And indeed, for the first time in many months, it was raining. At last the fields would grow food again! They all ran outside to feel the rain.

"I think it is my children who are magical," said Flora, hugging her son and daughter.

That night, as she was about to get into her hammock, Maria felt something in her pocket. It was the pouch of dolls she had spoken to the night before! But how had they gotten there? She was sure they had been sold to the mysterious man.

She opened the pouch. Inside with the dolls was a tiny piece of paper. It read: "Tell these dolls your secret wishes. Tell them your problems. Tell them your dreams. And when you awake, you may find the magic within you to make your dreams come true."

There was no signature—just a little stick drawing of a bearded man in a straw hat.

"Good night, my little friends," Maria whispered. "See you tomorrow."

And with that, Maria climbed into her hammock, lulled to sleep by the pit-pat-pit-pat sound of the rain.

how to use
your trouble dolls

A note to wish-makers: We cannot guarantee that your wishes will come true if you wish upon your trouble dolls. Nor can we guarantee that the dolls will solve your problems. But if you repeat your wishes every night and tell the dolls your troubles regularly, you may discover how to make your dreams come true. And you may also find that by telling the dolls your worries, your worries will be gone! When you share your worries with anyone, you often find that they are not as big as you thought they were before you spoke them. So keep wishing!

To Take Away Your Worries or Make Wishes—Traditional Method

Step 1. Spread your dolls out in front of you just before you go to sleep.

Step 2. Pick up a doll, close your eyes, and tell it one of your worries, or simply make a wish. It helps to explain why you are making the wish or what the problem is.

Step 3. Open your eyes and place the doll in the pouch.

Step 4. Repeat steps 2 and 3 as needed. You can make up to six wishes or tell your dolls six problems, one per doll.

Step 5. When your pouch is full of wishes and problems, place it beneath your pillow.

Step 6. Sleep tight! You may find that in the morning your worries are gone. Legend has it that in the night you will dream about how to solve your problems and how to make your wishes come true!

To Help a Friend or Family Member
If Your Friend or Family Member Is Present

Step 1. Spread your dolls out in front of you both just before you go to sleep.

Step 2. Pick up a doll, close your eyes, and explain to it that you want to help someone else with his or her problems or to make a wish come true. Open your eyes and place the doll beneath your pillow.

Step 3. Give the five remaining dolls to your friend or family member.

Step 4. Your friend can now tell each doll one problem or make one wish on each doll. Your friend can only make five wishes or tell the dolls five problems, one per doll. Make sure the person's eyes are closed when telling the dolls wishes or problems.

Step 5. When your friend has told the dolls what he or she wants to tell them, place the dolls in the pouch.

Step 6. Have your friend place the pouch beneath his or her pillow.

Step 7. Sleep tight! According to legend, your friend's worries may vanish, and you or your friend may dream about how to solve your friend's problems and how to make his or her wishes come true!

If Your Friend or Family Member Is Not Present

Repeat the traditional method, telling the dolls your friend's problems or wishes instead of your own. Place them in the pouch, as before, along with a small item or small photo given to you by your friend. If you cannot find an item small enough to fit in the pouch, place the item next to the pouch beneath your pillow and sleep tight. You or your friend should dream about what to do!

How to Make a Group Wish

Give five of your friends one doll each and keep one for yourself. Each person should hold the doll in his or her left hand. Tell everyone to stand in a circle and place his or her right hand on the shoulder of the person to the right. Close your eyes and make your wish together—you don't have to speak it out loud, but make sure that everyone is making the same wish. That night, everyone should sleep with the doll beneath his or her pillow. If you did it right, your wish may come true!

How to Make
Your Own Trouble Doll Bed

What You Need

A pair of scissors
A small, empty cardboard matchbox
Construction paper, colored or plain white
Glue or tape
A cotton ball
Markers, crayons, or colored pencils

Step 1. Remove the match tray.

Step 2. Cover matchbox with construction paper, leaving the openings uncovered. Cut the paper to fit.

Step 3. Take the paper off to decorate it if you wish. Look at the pictures and symbols in this book for traditional Guatemalan images, or use your own imagination.

Step 4. Tape or glue the paper to the outside of the matchbox.

Step 5. Pull little pieces of cotton from the cotton ball and fill the matchbox tray with them.

Step 6. Place the dolls on the cotton cushion and slide the tray in, sending your dolls to bed!

all about guatemala: where it is, what it's like

Your trouble dolls come from the amazing country of Guatemala, land of mountains and jungles, volcanoes and lakes, jaguars and beautifully colored birds. They were handmade by Maya people who live in this beautiful country. (The Maya are Native Central Americans who have lived in Guatemala for more than four thousand years!)

Guatemala is filled with the sights and sounds of ancient times. Quetzals fly through rain forests. Trees and flowers burst with color. The sun shines on ancient temples and with its shadows creates snakes that weave down the crumbling stairs.

What was life like in Guatemala during ancient times? How did the Maya live, and what did they believe? What is life like in Guatemala today? What do people do? What do they eat? How do they pass their days? And what would *your* life as a Guatemalan be like? Read on and find out....

But first, a few facts.

- Guatemala is a country that's just a bit larger than Ohio and a bit smaller than Tennessee. It is located in Central America, in between Mexico, Honduras, Belize, and El Salvador.
- The name "Guatemala" means the land of many trees, and indeed Guatemala is home to jungles, plains, beaches, volcanoes, and many, many trees.
- Guatemala's climate is tropical, but the weather in Guatemala depends on the region. In some areas the days are wet and cold, and at night the temperature drops below freezing, while in others it is usually very hot and humid.
- There are more than thirty active volcanoes in Guatemala. There have been three major volcanic eruptions in Guatemala—in 1773, 1917, and most recently in 1976. Here in the United

States, a country many times larger than Guatemala, we have had only one major eruption—Mount Saint Helens in Washington State in 1980.

- Hundreds of species of birds and animals live alongside the people of Guatemala. There are more than 600 different species of birds in Guatemala. There are only 650 different bird species in all of North America!

- The national bird of Guatemala is the quetzal. This beautiful bird has long, curving tail feathers of bright, shiny blue and green, and it is an important Maya symbol. In ancient times, the quetzal was thought to be the spiritual protector of chiefs—chiefs all wore quetzal feathers in their headdresses. Killing a quetzal was a capital offense, punishable by death.

- Other birds found in Guatemala include

beautiful tropical birds like the toucan, the parrot, and the macaw, white or pink flamingos, herons, and snowy egrets.

• Animals found in the jungles of Guatemala include the spider monkey, the howler monkey, the jaguar, the puma, many kinds of iguanas, the giant sea turtle, the coral snake, the tropical rattlesnake, the cayman (a type of crocodile), and giant bird-eating spiders!

The Ancient Maya—the First Guatemalans

According to most archaeologists, the scientists who study ancient cultures and the things they left behind, Guatemala was once the cultural center of the New World, many centuries before Columbus arrived. Archaeologists believe that the Maya civilization originated in Guatemala. The Maya eventually spread to present-day Guatemala, northern Belize, and Honduras. This part of Central America is known today as "Mundo Maya"—the Maya World.

Guatemala is a mix of ancient Maya tradition and modern Western influences. If you traveled there, you would find Maya people living in much the same way that their ancestors did thousands of years ago—using the same methods to make pots, weave cloth, cook food, and even build homes! Let's find out what that ancient Maya life was like.

Thus let it be done! Let the emptiness be filled!

Let the water recede and make a void.

Let the earth appear and become solid.

Let it be done.

Thus they spoke.

—*"The Creation," from the* **Popol Vuh,**
the sacred book of the Maya

The Great Maya Civilization

The Maya civilization was once very impressive. When Europe was still in the Dark Ages, the period of time from 500–1000 C.E. when it was in chaos and when almost no important art or science was created, the Maya had already mapped the heavens accurately, created the only writing system native to the Americas (North, Central, and South) and were masters of mathematics. They were good farmers and built elaborate underground reservoirs to store water for times of drought. They erected beautiful and highly decorated buildings, temples, pyramids, palaces, and astronomical observatories—all without the use of metal tools, help from strong animals like oxen, or even the basic wheel!

How the First Guatemalans Lived

The Maya civilization was ruled by nobles and kings who lived in beautiful palaces, while most people lived in small villages. Families lived in small one-room huts, with walls made of dried mud and wooden poles and a roof made of palm leaves. The huts were used mainly for sleeping and for shelter from the rain—most of the time was spent outdoors weaving, farming, and cooking in a central village compound. People were organized by the role they played in society, which was determined by the role their parents played and their parents before them, and so on. Kings were, of course, at the top, followed (in order) by nobles,

teachers, scribes (writers who recorded everything, from history to religion to science), warriors, architects, administrators, craftspeople, merchants, workers, and farmers.

Maya Beliefs and Religion

For all of their skills in science, art, writing, and math, the Maya also had some odd beliefs and practices.

- The Maya believed that the earth was four-cornered and flat.

- Some Maya believed that this flat world was supported by four gods, one at each corner. Other Maya thought this was silly. They knew that the world was supported by four trees, one at each corner. (The ceiba, the national tree of Guatemala, was at the center of the world.) And other Maya thought the world was the back of a giant crocodile resting in a pool (the ocean).

- The Maya did not believe in only one god—in fact, they believed that there were 166 gods governing the world, the heavens, and the underworld. Each day, the gods died and were reborn as the sun set and rose.

- The Maya believed that bloodletting was necessary to keep the gods happy and to encourage everything from rain to success in war. The king sometimes pierced his tongue with a sharp knife or stingray spine and let his blood flow onto the ground in order to win the favor of the gods.

- Human sacrifice was also practiced in ancient Maya culture to win the favor of the gods for upcoming battles, a new ruler, or other significant events. It was considered an honor to be chosen for human sacrifice. Would you be honored?

- The ancient Maya considered a flattened forehead to be a sign of beauty. If you were born to Maya parents in ancient times, your parents would have tied two boards to your forehead while your skull bones were still soft. This would cause your head to become longer and angled back instead of straight up and down. (Luckily, when you are an infant, your brain is pretty pliable, so this wouldn't have made you any less intelligent!)

- Another sign of Maya beauty was crossed eyes. Your parents might have dangled a bead of wax in front of your eyes from birth. You would have become permanently cross-eyed from looking at it! (Don't try this at home with your baby brother or sister.)

- Maya women also sharpened their teeth into fangs, and both men and women had their teeth decorated with jade or obsidian.

Maya Games

It wasn't all work and human sacrifice for the ancient Maya—they also played games. A popular Maya sport was hip ball, which

was a sort of combination tennis, baseball, soccer, and basketball games. Today in Guatemala, you can still walk on the stone courts where this sport was played if you visit the ancient Maya ruins.

Hip-ball players used a hard rubber ball and possibly a wooden bat. Players had to keep the ball in the air and couldn't let it hit the ground. They did this by batting it with any part of their bodies except their hands, feet, and head.

This game was often used to settle arguments and fights between tribes.

However, hip ball wasn't just a friendly game. In some games, players played to the death. The captain of the losing team was killed or sacrificed in a religious ceremony. Today, the most popular games in Guatemala are football (soccer) and that American pastime, baseball. Don't worry—no one plays to the death anymore!

Ancient Maya Numbers

The ancient Maya were extremely advanced both in their written and oral language. In fact, they developed the concept of zero, something the Romans never did.

Ancient Maya numbers were very similar to our numbers. However, instead of counting in groups of ten (decimal system based on *deci*, ten) like we do, they counted them in groups of twenty (vigesimal system). So instead of just using fingers to learn how to count, Maya children used fingers and toes. This meant that large numbers were written in groups of twenty. For instance, in our decimal system, we write the number 32 as $3 \times 10 + 2$. In the Maya system, this would be $1 \times 20 + 12$.

Where Did the Maya Go?

The Maya people are still around, but the civilization itself died out in 900 C.E. No one knows exactly how or why—perhaps the Maya were invaded by a nearby culture. This may have left them open to conquest when the Spanish arrived in 1521 C.E.

The Spaniards easily took control of Mundo Maya in 1530 C.E., killing millions of people and destroying almost all of the records of the civilization. But the Maya left us a written legacy of their society that the Spanish did not destroy. Tall stelae, or carved stones, stand in many former Maya centers. The writing tells the stories of Maya history, rulers, battles, and even marriages. Luckily, archaeologists found the translation key, and we can now read what these ancient Maya wrote.

How to Speak Maya
Pronunciation Guide

a.....“ah” as in “calm”

e.....“eh” as in “effort”

i.....“ee” as in “seen”

o.....“oh” as in “open”

oo.....same sound as “o” but held longer

u.....“oo” as in “moon”

x.....“sh” as in “bush”

c is always hard like “k”

j is always a hard “h” sound

Common Phrases

English	Spanish	Maya
Hi, how are you?	¿Hola, cómo está?	Bix a belex?
Fine (or okay)	Muy bien	Maloob
Thank you	Gracias	Yum botic
You're welcome	De nada.	Mixba.
Where are you going?	¿Dónde están?	Tu'x ka binex?

the people of guatemala today

Today, two thirds of all Guatemalans are of Maya descent. Most Maya today practice a religion and a way of life that mixes ancient Maya ideas, a belief in the sacredness of animals and nature, and Catholicism. Some Maya still see their village as the ancient Maya saw the world—as supported by four gods in the corners. When one of these gods becomes upset, the god shifts his position and causes an earthquake. The Maya today also believe in the supernatural spirits of the forest and often pray to the jaguar to keep evil away.

- If you lived in Guatemala today, you'd be living with twelve million other people from a variety of ethnic origins. The majority of the people are either Maya Indians or Latino people.
- Unfortunately, Guatemala is one of the poorest countries in Central America and even in the world. The average family earns $944 per year. The United States is ranked ninth in wealth, and its average family income is $44,568. What a difference!

- Most Guatemalans (two thirds of the people) live in rural areas that are outside cities and towns, usually without electricity or running water.
- Only 56 percent of all Guatemalans can read. Most of these are men—95 percent of Maya women can't read. In the United States, 95 percent of women and 96 percent of men *can* read.
- If you lived in Guatemala, it is very likely that you would come from a family of farmers. Guatemala has land that is very good for farming because its volcanoes heat the soil and land from inside, and this creates a "greenhouse effect." This allows people to plant and harvest crops year-round.

What Guatemalans Wear

Today, traditional clothing in Guatemala, or *traje indígena*, is not so different from clothing worn centuries ago.

Maya women and girls wear a *huipil*, a type of blouse or tunic made by folding a cloth in two and cutting an opening for the head.

Guatemalan Social Customs

There are many differences between Guatemalan culture and our own. Here are a few of them.

- Politeness is very important in Guatemala. It is considered rude not to greet someone you pass on the street.

- Many people shake hands when they see each other, although these handshakes are usually very lightweight—what we would call a "dead fish" handshake.

- Most Guatemalans speak very slowly, in very soft tones. Guatemalans are taken aback if you speak too loudly and they have a hard time understanding you if you speak too fast! So if you visit, don't yell!

- The Maya are traditionally very respectful of their elders. When Maya children see their grandparents, for example, they often kiss their hands and bow to them! (Try this the next time you see yours—they might like it.)

- Most Guatemalans get from place to place by walking, taking buses, or hitchhiking. Wealthier Guatemalans may have their own vehicles—but usually a motorcycle or scooter, not a car.

The word *huipil* comes from an Aztec phrase meaning "my covering." Women's skirts, or *córte,* are made of cloth that is seven to ten yards long, wrapped around the body. Girls wear their skirts above the knees, married women at the knees, and old women below the knees.

Today, fewer Guatemalan men than women wear traditional clothing. If you went there, you'd see a lot of boys and men wearing blue jeans. But men and boys also wear traditional clothing, usually shirts with a heavily embroidered collar, and baggy pants. Some men wear long, baggy shorts.

Both men and women wear *faja*— waist sashes to hold up their skirts or pants. Many Guatemalans carry a large cloth called a *sute* that can be used as a head covering, a baby sling, a bag for food, a basket cover, or a shawl.

And ordinary folks still wear hats—the bigger the hat, the more important the head.

Many Guatemalans today go barefoot or wear *caites*, sandals with soles made from old rubber tires. These sandals are popular from time to time in the United States.

The Importance of Weaving

Weaving is still one of the most important skills in Guatemala. If you lived there, your mother would teach you how to weave at a very young age, just as her mother would have taught her, just as your great-grandmother would have taught your grandmother, and so on. Many families weave their own cloth for clothing, blankets, pouches, and hammocks—cloth just like the cloth on your dolls. The Maya still weave on the backstrap loom, the same basic loom

they have used for centuries. They believe it was a gift from Ix Chel, the goddess of childbirth and healing, to Maya women.

Living Jewelry

Once upon a time, according to legend,
there was a Maya princess who fell in love with a man
she was not allowed to marry. She wept night and day
over her forbidden love. A shaman heard her cries,
and, learning of her misery, he turned her into
a shining beetle—a piece of living jewelry. She spent
the rest of her life pinned to the breast of her beloved,
right above his heart.

Today, the Maya decorate living beetles
with rhinestones and tie them to a little gold leash.
These living beetles are then pinned to some lucky
person's chest and spend the rest of their lives walking back
and forth, sparkling as they move.

The Guatemalan people have always worn very colorful and decorative clothing. Designs like flowers, snakes, frogs, corn, double-headed eagles, and diamonds have mystical importance to them and are featured on their clothing, blankets, and wall hangings. Many of the designs are centuries old, and the patterns are found on ancient stelae, the standing, carved stone monuments found in Maya ruins. Different villages and families wear different patterns in their clothing. In Guatemala alone, there are at least 500 different designs!

Going to Market

Most villagers go to local markets once or twice a week to buy and sell everyday items such as clothing, food, and supplies for the home. This is an old tradition, and many of these markets have been operating in the same locations and taking place on the same days of the week for hundreds of years.

If you went to a market, you could buy everything from food to clothing, from crafts and artwork to practical items like pots and pans. You would expect to spend a long time negotiating with the sellers. Bargaining is expected and is part of the fun of market day.

Money

Guatemalan money is divided like dollars and cents. There are a hundred *centavos* (C) in a *quetzal* (Q). In recent years, you could trade one US dollar for seven *quetzals*. This exchange rate goes up and down daily. One Q is also called a *billete* (bill) or *sencillo* (single). Just like the buck!

Here's what some everyday items cost in Guatemala.

candy bars: 10 *quetzals* (about $1.50—because they have to be imported, or brought in)

cars: 70,000–210,000 *quetzals* (about as much as they cost here— they have to be imported)

cookie: 50 *centavos* (about $.07)

cup of *atole*: 1 *quetzal* (about $.15)

dinner: 20 *quetzals* in a restaurant (about $3); 5–10 *quetzals* at the market ($.75–$1.50) houses: 140,000–700,000 *quetzals* in Guatemala City

    ($20,000–$100,000); 35,000 *quetzals* in rural areas ($5,000)

ice cream scoop: 1–3 *quetzals* (about $.15–$.45)

movie ticket: 6 *quetzals* (about $.80)

pants: 150 *quetzals* (about $20)

sash: 80 *quetzals* (about $11)

shirt: 120 *quetzals* (about $16)

Guatemalan Foods

Corn, or maize, has been the main food in the Guatemalan diet since

ancient times. Most ancient meals included corn tamales or tortillas and, at breakfast, a hot corn drink called *atole*. Chocolate is available in Guatemala, but in ancient times it was considered a "drink of the gods" and only the royalty and nobility were allowed to drink it. Today, people in Guatemala and Mexico still drink a chocolate

version of the *atole* drink.
(See page 52 to make your own chocolate *atole*.)

If you lived in Guatemala, you would help your mother grind corn every day to make tortillas (thin pancakes) and other basic foods. Your home would have the supplies needed to prepare the maize: the *metate,* a grinding stone (a slab of black rock with three legs that slopes downward), the *metlapil* (a roller made of the same stone), and the *banqueta* and *banquillo* (the wooden table and stool used to make the *masa,* the ground corn mixture used in cooking). It is very likely that every meal you ate would include some type of corn product—either tamales (cornmeal cooked in banana leaves), tortillas, or *atole.* Often, corn tortillas are all Guatemalan families have to eat.

A Typical Guatemalan Menu
Breakfast
huevos y frijoles: eggs and black beans

Lunch
tamales: banana leaf with steamed maize paste inside,
sometimes with vegetables or bits of meat
chuchitos: cornmeal dumplings stuffed with meat

Dinner
pejelagarto: alligator-headed fish seasoned with chile and lemon
ceviche: raw fish, shrimp, lobster, squid, or conch
chipped and marinated in lime juice, which "cooks" it

Dessert
plátanos fritos: fried bananas

How to Make *Atole de Chocolate*

NOTE: This recipe requires the use of a blender and a stove,
so get your parents to help you!

Makes 1 quart or 5 servings

½ can corn niblets, drained (or ½ cup frozen corn niblets)

2 cups milk

3.3-ounce bar of unsweetened chocolate, chopped

⅓ cup dark brown sugar, packed

½ tablespoon molasses

a few anise seeds, crushed (optional)

1. Measure 1¾ cups water into a blender or food processor.
   Add the corn. Blend until smooth. Pour into a medium-
   size saucepan.
2. Add the milk, chocolate, brown sugar, molasses, and optional
   anise seeds. Over medium heat, bring to a simmer, whisking
   constantly. Simmer, whisking frequently, until the chocolate,
   sugar, and molasses are completely dissolved (about 5 minutes).
3. Strain, if you wish. Serve in cups or mugs.

Daily Life in Guatemala

Life for today's Maya families in Guatemala is backbreaking work. Men, women, and children must all work constantly to live. You would have a lot of daily chores, from picking and planting food to gathering wood, grinding corn, and cleaning. (Maybe doing the dishes and cleaning your room doesn't sound so bad after all.)

Maya families spend much of their time growing, selling, and obtaining food. Once or twice a week, families walk several hours to market and several hours home, all for a few *centavos* of profit. Families spend an equal amount of time gathering wood to heat their homes (since there is no electricity or natural gas, they heat their homes with a large central fire). Every day, a typical family walks two

Guatemala Factoid:

The ancient Maya ate dogs. They thought that the tastiest dog meat came from dogs that were vegetarians. The Spanish eventually got used to this custom, and when Spanish sailors sailed from the New World back to Spain, the ships often stocked salted dog meat for the sailors to eat on the way home.

Guatemala Factoid:

Residents of Antigua are called *panza verde*, meaning "green belly," because they eat so many avocados.

Guatemala Factoid:
Got Any Gum?

Guatemala was one of the first places in the world to have chewing gum. Chicle is the sap from the chicozapote tree, found in the Petèn region of Guatemala. This tree sap is what gum is made from! Guatemala is still one of the suppliers of chicle to gum makers around the world.

hours down the mountain, spends eight hours gathering wood, and travels three hours back up the mountain with a heavy load of *lena*, or firewood.

Another important task is obtaining water. Getting water usually means going to the closest well or stream and bringing back pots of water. Many trips are needed each day to get enough water for one family. How many clay pots of water per day do you think your family would need? Don't forget washing dishes and clothes, baths, and brushing teeth.

Guatemalan Homes

Ancient Maya families lived in houses called *xanil nah*, the thatched huts made of mud and wood described earlier. Many of today's Guatemalan families live in similar huts. If you were a Maya, you would build your home the same way your ancestors did, with the help of friends and family.

First, you'd lay a stone foundation and then top it with a frame of poles from stripped young trees. You would build two doorways on opposite sides of the house to allow the air to flow. Then you'd fill in the frame with poles or stucco. Finally, you'd add a thick roof of palm thatch. If you

wanted to be really modern, you might add cinder block or cement for the walls and metal or tar paper for the roof. And now you're ready to move in. But don't plan on bringing a bed—most Maya sleep in hammocks!

Kids' Life in Guatemala

Life for children in Guatemala is no easier than it is for adults. Children work along with their parents to gather wood and food, starting at a young age—four or five. The modern Maya often find work as migrant workers. This means that families move to different areas depending on the season and which crop needs to be picked.

The Turtle Race

From September to December, every Saturday in Monterrico, Guatemala, a special race takes place. Workers from the Tortugario Monterrico (the Monterrico Turtle Sanctuary) come to the beach with plastic tubs and two long ropes. They place one rope high on the beach, away from the water. Standing behind the rope, they each hold a baby turtle, and when the whistle blows, they let the turtles go. The baby turtles run as fast as they can to the sea. The turtles are released in groups so more of them have a chance to reach the sea and survive. Because turtles are creatures of habit and this is their first exposure to the sea, they remember the location of the race—later, when they are adults, they will return to this exact place to lay their eggs.

Carry That Weight

If you were a Guatemalan, you would learn how to carry heavy loads the same way your ancestors have carried them for centuries—on your back. You would see people of all ages carrying firewood, food, live animals, dead animals, and a lot of other items. The Guatemalans tie a strap around whatever they are carrying, loop it over their head, and rest the weight on their back. (Scientists know Guatemalans have carried things this way for years because the skeletons of the ancient dead have the same spinal deformities as those of modern Maya!)

Going to school is required in Guatemala between the ages of seven and fourteen. All Guatemalan schools are free, but only eight out of ten children actually go to elementary school, and only two out of ten go on to high school. If you were a Maya child, school would be

twice as hard, at first. You would show up on the first day and not even speak the language the teacher was speaking. You'd have to learn Spanish first to know what was going on.

The school year in Guatemala is very different from ours. School begins on January 15 and ends on October 15. This doesn't mean there is no summer vacation, however—Guatemala's dry season (summer) runs from the end of October to the end of December.

Guatemala Factoid: Soccer, not Nintendo, is the most popular game in Guatemala. But not every kid can afford a ball. If you lived there, you might have to make friends with a neighbor who had his or her own ball. This isn't difficult, though—people are very friendly.

How to Carry Your Books, Guatemalan Style
What You Need:

A strap of cloth about six inches wide and at least five feet long

A pile of books

Step 1. Place your books in a pile on the floor.

Step 2. Tie the strap around the pile as if you were wrapping ribbon on a present. The strap should go once around the middle of the pile, right to left, and once around the middle of the pile, top to bottom. Tie it nice and tight so the books won't fall out on your way to school.

Step 3. Tie the ends of the strap together.

Step 4. Twist the strap once to make a loop at the top that is big enough to fit your head.

Step 5. Bend down in front of the pile and place your head through the loop, resting the strap around the top of your head like a headband. When you stand, your books should be hanging off your back, with their weight on your forehead. Now try walking to school like that every day!

rabbit and coyote: a maya folktale

Coyote was always trying to catch Rabbit. But every time Coyote was close to capturing Rabbit and having a nice, tasty dinner, Rabbit found a way to outwit him.

One night, Rabbit was very tired. He'd had a long day and was sleeping next to a lake. Coyote came upon him and grabbed him.

"Now I've got you!" said Coyote.

Rabbit, calm as ever, said, "Don't be silly, Coyote. You don't want to eat me."

Coyote scratched his head. "Yes, I think I do." And he opened his mouth to swallow Rabbit.

"No, you don't," said Rabbit. "Wouldn't you rather have that great cheese at the bottom of the lake?" And with his ear, he pointed to the middle of the lake, where indeed there appeared to be a big, round cheese!

Coyote licked his lips. "It has been a while since I've had cheese," he said. And with that, he released Rabbit and swam to the middle of the lake for the cheese. But when he got there, he couldn't find it.

"I see the cheese reflected in the water," said Coyote. "But I cannot grasp it."

Rabbit just laughed. "That's because there is no cheese—it's just the reflection of the moon."

Coyote looked up and saw that indeed the moon was shining down on the lake, looking very much like a big wheel of cheese.

"Enjoy your meal," said Rabbit, "for I will take no part in it tonight!" And with that, he hopped away before Coyote could swim back to shore.